2/03

W9-CKW-507

Turkeys on the Farm

by Mari C. Schuh

Consulting Editor: Gail Saunders-Smith, Ph.D.

Consultant: Cary J. Trexler, Assistant Professor,
Department of Agricultural Education and Studies,
Iowa State University

Pebble Books

an imprint of Capstone Press
Mankato, Minnesota

Pebble Books are published by Capstone Press
151 Good Counsel Drive, P.O. Box 669, Mankato, Minnesota 56002
http://www.capstone-press.com

1 2 3 4 5 6 07 06 05 04 03 02

Library of Congress Cataloging-in-Publication Data
Schuh, Mari C., 1975–
    Turkeys on the farm / by Mari C. Schuh.
    p. cm.—(On the farm)
    Includes bibliographical references (p. 23) and index.
    Summary: Simple text and photographs describe turkeys and their life
on the farm.
    ISBN 0-7368-1190-7
    1. Turkeys—Juvenile literature. [1. Turkeys.] I. Title. II. Series.
SF507 .S34 2002
636.5'92—dc21   2001003226

Note to Parents and Teachers

The On the Farm series supports national science standards related
to life science. This book describes and illustrates turkeys and their
lives on the farm. The photographs support early readers in
understanding the text. The repetition of words and phrases helps
early readers learn new words. This book also introduces early
readers to subject-specific vocabulary words, which are defined
in the Words to Know section. Early readers may need assistance
to read some words and to use the Table of Contents, Words to
Know, Read More, Internet Sites, and Index/Word List sections
of the book.

Table of Contents

tail

feathers

beak

wattle

Turkeys are farm animals. Most farm turkeys are large birds with white feathers.

wattle

A turkey's head is
bald and bumpy.
A red wattle grows
on a turkey's neck.

Most turkeys live
on large farms.
Some turkeys live
on small farms.

Farmers raise turkeys for their meat.

Farmers keep
turkey barns clean.

Farmers feed corn and soybean meal to turkeys. Farmers also give a lot of water to turkeys.

Turkeys raised on farms cannot fly. But they can run very fast.

hen

tom

18

A female turkey is a hen.
A male turkey is a tom.

Toms gobble.

Words to Know

bald—without hair or fur

bumpy—very uneven; turkeys have bumpy heads.

gobble—to make a sound like a turkey; only male turkeys gobble.

meat—the flesh of an animal that can be eaten

raise—to care for animals as they grow and become older

soybean—a seed that grows in pods on bushy plants; farmers feed turkeys a corn and soybean meal mixture that has vitamins and minerals; meal is ground up food, vitamins, and minerals.

wattle—folds of skin under a turkey's neck; turkeys cannot sweat; wattles help them get rid of heat.

Read More

Arnosky, Jim. *All about Turkeys.* New York: Scholastic Press, 1998.

Bell, Rachael. *Turkeys.* Farm Animals. Chicago: Heinemann Library, 2000.

Hoare, Ben. *Turkeys.* Nature's Children. Danbury, Conn.: Grolier Educational, 2001.

Internet Sites

All about Turkeys for Kids
http://kiddyhouse.com/farm/Turkeys

Kids Farm: Turkeys
http://www.kidsfarm.com/turkeys.htm

Turkey
http://www.enchantedlearning.com/
subjects/birds/printouts/Turkeyprintout.shtml

Index/Word List

animals, 5
bald, 7
barns, 13
birds, 5
bumpy, 7
clean, 13
corn, 15
farm, 5, 9, 17
farmers, 11,
    13, 15
fast, 17
feathers, 5

feed, 15
female, 19
fly, 17
give, 15
gobble, 21
grows, 7
head, 7
hen, 19
keep, 13
large, 5, 9
live, 9
male, 19

meat, 11
neck, 7
raise, 11, 17
red, 7
run, 17
small, 9
soybean meal,
    15
tom, 19, 21
water, 15
wattle, 7
white, 5

Word Count: 94
Early-Intervention Level: 11

Credits
Heather Kindseth, cover designer; Heidi Meyer, production designer;
    Kimberly Danger and Deirdre Barton, photo researchers

Capstone Press/Jim Foell, 4, 12, 18 (both)
David F. Clobes Stock Photography, 1, 10, 14
International Stock/Bob Firth, 16
Photo Network, 8 (bottom); Tom Campbell, 8 (top)
Unicorn Stock Photos/James L. Fly, 20
Visuals Unlimited/Inga Spence, cover, 6